GW01237439

Challenge
English
KS2: Year 6
Age 10–11

Louis Fidge

Text and illustrations © Hodder Education

First published in 2007
exclusively for WHSmith by
Hodder Education, an Hachette UK Company,
338 Euston Road
London NW1 3BH

Impression number   10 9 8 7 6 5
Year   2011

Cover illustration by Sally Newton Illustrations

Typeset by Servis Filmsetting Ltd, Stockport, Cheshire

Printed and bound in Spain

A CIP record for this book is available from the British Library

ISBN: 978 0 340 94549 0

Parents' notes

How this series can help your child

- The *WHS Challenge* series provides a wide range of activities that will stretch and challenge your child.
- It offers a straightforward, no-nonsense approach to basic English skills.
- It is carefully graded and provides a continuous development of essential English skills throughout Key Stage 2.
- There is comprehensive coverage of the skills that form part of the National Curriculum.
- Regular tests are included so progress and achievement can clearly be seen.
- The series gives your child confidence to face the different types of tests in school.
- It helps to improve your child's results in school.
- It is designed to be used alongside any English course your child is using.
- Its clear, accessible format offers rigour, support and structure.

Using this book

- There are 24 topics and 4 tests in the book. A test occurs after 6 topics have been completed.
- Each topic need not be completed in one session. Think of it as about a week's work.
- Do give help and encouragement. Completing the activities should not become a chore.
- Do let your child mark his or her own work under your supervision and correct any careless mistakes he or she might have made.
- When all the tests have been completed let your child fill in the Certificate of Achievement on the opposite page.
- Each double page has a title, explanation of the learning point, practice section, and challenge section.

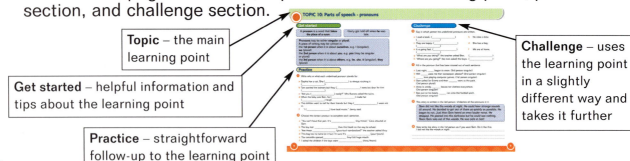

Topic – the main learning point

Get started – helpful information and tips about the learning point

Practice – straightforward follow-up to the learning point

Challenge – uses the learning point in a slightly different way and takes it further

This certifies
that

_____

has completed

CHALLENGE ENGLISH YEAR 6

on _____

Scoring _____ on TEST 1

_____ on TEST 2

_____ on TEST 3

and _____ on TEST 4

Total score
out of 100 _____   40–50   good effort
50–60   well done
60–70   fantastic
70–100   brilliant

Topic 1: Common letter strings

Get started

It is helpful to look for **common letter strings** in groups of words.

Identifying common letter strings will help you spell other words.

consider**ate**		chocol**ate**

Tom was very consider**ate**. He gave his mum some chocol**ate** for her birthday.

Practice

1 Make some words with common letter strings.

a

```
                              ┌──────────┐
                              │   ate    │
                              └──────────┘
illust**rate**    educ___    chocol___    separ___    deliber___    consider___

__illustrate__    _____    _____    _____    _____    _____
```

b

```
                              ┌──────────┐
                              │   ete    │
                              └──────────┘
athl____    comp____    compl____    del____    concr____    obsol____

_____    _____    _____    _____    _____    _____
```

c

```
                              ┌──────────┐
                              │   ite    │
                              └──────────┘
defin____    favour____    dynam____    oppos____    pol____    rec____

_____    _____    _____    _____    _____    _____
```

Challenge

2 Match up the pairs of words with the same letter strings.

Write them here. Underline the common letter strings.

factory	arrogant
fragrant	hedgehog
fruit	touch
warehouse	story
badge	burgle
beaten	bruise
tongue	antique
crouch	sweaty
disturb	catalogue
plaque	scared

_____

_____

_____

fact<u>ory</u>   st<u>ory</u>

_____

_____

_____

_____

_____

_____

3 Underline the common letter string in each pair of words.
Think of one other word that contains the same letter string.

inspector	collector	_____	burglar	vicar	_____
nature	picture	_____	through	rough	_____
police	office	_____	musical	legal	_____
famous	nervous	_____	possess	princess	_____
naughty	laughter	_____	observance	dance	_____
pedestrian	librarian	_____	splendour	vapour	_____
volunteer	engineer	_____	spectacle	miracle	_____

Get started

a **teacher** in a **library** with a **book**

My name is **Leroy**. I come from **London**. Have you seen **Big Ben**?

A butterfly is a thing of **beauty**.

A **common noun** is a **general name** of a **person**, a **place** or a **thing**.

A **proper noun** is the **particular name** of a **person**, a **place** or a **thing**. Proper nouns begin with **capital letters**.

Abstract nouns are names of **thoughts**, **ideas** and **feelings**. You **cannot** touch, taste, see, hear or smell them.

Practice

1 Write the common nouns in the wall in the correct column in the chart.

doctor	dock	orange	astronaut
moon	hangar	lorry	dentist
cup	bank	carpenter	library
pencil	church	computer	stadium
plumber	leaf	editor	factory

names of people	names of places	names of things

Challenge

2 **Rewrite these sentences. Punctuate them correctly.**
Underline the proper nouns.

a mount kilimanjaro is the highest mountain in africa

_____

b edinburgh is the capital city of scotland

_____

c I bought a copy of the daily mirror and the tv times

_____

d yesterday was thursday the first day of december

_____

e sir francis drake was a sailor in the reign of queen elizabeth the first

_____

f we went to the gaumont cinema in luton

_____

3 **Use the abstract nouns in the box to complete the sentences.**

| fear | strength | poverty | speed | courage | belief |

a The weightlifter seemed to possess enormous _____.

b The child showed great _____ when he had an operation.

c Many people have no money and live in complete _____.

d I was filled with _____ when I saw the hairy monster.

e The car was going at such great _____ it could not stop in time.

f It is my _____ that one day the world will live in peace.

Topic 3: Double letters

stop – sto**pp**ing

carry

begin – begi**nn**er

Rule 1
In words with **one syllable** containing a **short vowel** in the **middle**, we must **double** the **final consonant** before adding a **suffix beginning** with a **vowel**.

Rule 2
Consonants are often **doubled** after the **first syllable** of a word **if** the first syllable contains a **short vowel** sound.

Rule 3
In words of **more** than **one** syllable, if the **last** syllable contains a **short vowel** and **ends** with a **single consonant**, we must **double** the **final consonant** before adding a **suffix beginning** with a **vowel**.

Practice

1. Make some new words by adding a suffix to the end of all of the words you can.

   You will not be able to add every suffix to every word.

root word	+ suffix **er**	+ suffix **est**	+ suffix **ing**	+ suffix **ed**
hop	hopper		hopping	hopped
skip				
bat				
hum				
sad				
fit				
plan				
jog				
hot				
flat				
big				
ban				
but				
wet				

Challenge

2 **Choose one of these pairs of letters to complete each word.**

rr	nn	mm	bb	ss

a te_**rr**_or   b a____ive   c ba____er   d ba____ow

e di____er   f ri____on   g le____on   h me____age

i flu____y   j ca____y   k co____on   l ma____iage

m su____er   n ru____age   o ra____it   p bo____ow

q ha____er   r bu____ow   s ca____iage   t ho____or

3 **Now break each word into two syllables.**

a __ter__ / __ror__   b ____ / ____   c ____ / ____   d ____ / ____

e ____ / ____   f ____ / ____   g ____ / ____   h ____ / ____

i ____ / ____   j ____ / ____   k ____ / ____   l ____ / ____

m ____ / ____   n ____ / ____   o ____ / ____   p ____ / ____

q ____ / ____   r ____ / ____   s ____ / ____   t ____ / ____

4 **Mark these spellings. There are ten mistakes.**
Correct the words that are wrong.

a refitted ☐   b omiting ☐   c marvelous ☐   d occurrence ☐

e labelled ☐   f deterent ☐   g rebelion ☐   h inferred ☐

i admitted ☐   j traveler ☐   k recurring ☐   l forgoten ☐

m permiting ☐   n signaller ☐   o metalic ☐   p quarrelled ☐

q cancellation ☐   r incuring ☐   s regretted ☐   t leveled ☐

Topic 4: Parts of speech – verbs

Get started

Verbs may be written in different tenses.

Yesterday I **ate** an apple (**past tense**).
Now I **eat** an apple (**present tense**).
Tomorrow I **will eat** an apple (**future tense**).

Sometimes we use an **auxiliary** (or **helper**) verb with the main verb.

The auxiliary verb gives us **information** about the **tense** of the verb.

I **am** swimming (present tense).
I **was** swimming (past tense).
I **will** swim (future tense).

Practice

1 Indicate whether the verb in each of these sentences is in the past tense (P), present tense (Pr) or future tense (F).

a I eat my dinner. (___) b Yesterday it rained all day. (___)

c Will you come shopping? (___) d I feel excited. (___)

e For my birthday I got a bike. (___) f We will win the cup next week. (___)

g The boy watches TV. (___) h My mum drank her coffee. (___)

i Tom will be eleven next June. (___) j That dog barks too much. (___)

k We went home. (___) l I will have a bath soon. (___)

m The sun shines. (___) n You got all your maths wrong. (___)

o Next week I will be in Spain. (___) p At the moment I'm very hot. (___)

Challenge

2 Underline the auxiliary verb in each sentence.
Indicate whether the sentence is written in the past tense (P),
present tense (Pr) or future tense (F).

a Edward <u>is</u> drinking. (**Pr**)

b My mother was humming. (___)

c I am reading a book. (___)

d The children were playing. (___)

e I will see you later. (___)

f I have travelled in a plane. (___)

g Sarah has climbed the tree. (___)

h I will try harder tomorrow. (___)

i My cat is purring. (___)

j The dog was gnawing a bone. (___)

k William is smiling. (___)

l My friend was swimming. (___)

m I am doing some homework. (___)

n The children were arguing. (___)

o I will call for you tomorrow. (___)

p I have been to Italy. (___)

3 One of the auxiliary verbs in the box has been missed out of each
sentence. Mark where you think it should go and write it in.

should	would	could	might

a If you are tired you ^should go to bed.

b I buy the video game if I had enough money.

c I cross the road if it wasn't so busy.

d I told you that if you practised you get better.

e If horses had wings they fly!

f You not stay out in direct sunshine too long.

g I not eat my dinner because it was cold.

h I be grateful if you helped me.

i If I buy a ticket I win.

j If it rains tomorrow, I get wet.

11

Topic 5: Prefixes

Get started

A **prefix** is a **group of letters** that is added to the **beginning** of a word.

Prefixes often have a **particular meaning**.

bi means **two** as in the word **bi**noculars

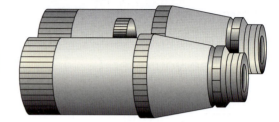

Practice

1 **Add the prefix to each word. Write the word you make.**

a auto + mobile = _____
b bi + lingual = _____

c dis + agree = _____
d extra + ordinary = _____

e il + legal = _____
f inter + view = _____

g micro + scope = _____
h aqua + plane = _____

i sub + marine = _____
j super + human = _____

k pre + historic = _____
l centi + metre = _____

m dis + appear = _____
n bi + cycle = _____

o sur + plus = _____
p in + land = _____

q semi + circle = _____
r out + do = _____

s un + well = _____
t ex + port = _____

Challenge

2 Write a definition for each word. Use a dictionary if necessary.

prefix	meaning of prefix	word	definition
in	opposite of	**in**secure	
tri	three	**tri**angle	
semi	half	**semi**circle	
non	not	**non**sense	
post	after, behind	**post**script	
mis	bad, wrong	**mis**behave	
re	again	**re**play	
peri	around	**peri**meter	
under	beneath	**under**current	
with	back	**with**draw	
equi	equal	**equi**lateral	

3 Find two words beginning with each prefix. Write what you think the prefix means. Use a dictionary if necessary.

prefix	two words beginning with the prefix		meaning of the prefix
anti	antiseptic	antibiotic	against
aero			
geo			
tele			
super			
mono			
auto			
multi			
mini			
uni			
inter			
ex			
fore			

Topic 6: Parts of speech – adjectives

Get started

a **haunted** house

The woman **with the curly hair** sat down.

Adjectives are **describing** words. They give us **more information** about **nouns**.

An **adjectival phrase** does the same job as an **adjective**. It **describes a noun**.

Practice

1 **Find and underline the adjectives in the sentences.**

a The weather was sunny and hot.

b The huge crowd watched a thrilling game.

c Anna was hungry, Paul was tired and James was thirsty.

d The old woman lived in a little, thatched cottage.

e The ancient sailor raised his bony hand.

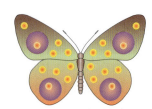

f The magnificent butterfly had beautiful patterns on its wings.

g The first car was a brilliant red colour.

h The shaggy, black dog was eating a juicy bone.

i Jenna wore a rough, woollen scarf.

j The mountaineers were weary and disheartened.

k The alien spoke in a strange, metallic voice.

Challenge

2 Sort out the adjectives in the wall into four sets.

	scared	huge	sweet	red	amazed	
thin	brown	salty	bored	yellow	short
silver	tall	happy	spicy	sour	

adjectives to do with:			
colour	**size**	**feelings**	**taste**

3 Think of one more adjective for each set. Write each one in the chart above.

4 Make up some sentences of your own. Use the following adjectival phrases in your sentences.

with long floppy ears	tired but happy	all slippery and slimy
clean-shaven	long and tangled	out of breath

_____

_____

_____

_____

_____

_____

Test 1 (Score 1 mark for every correct answer.)

 Topic 1

Underline the common letter string in each set of words.

1. factory · · · history · · · observatory
2. antique · · · unique · · · plaque
3. burglar · · · vicar · · · sugar
4. office · · · mice · · · twice

Topic 2

Fill in the missing vowels in these abstract nouns.

5. kn___wl___dg___ · · · · · · 6. ___xp___ct___t___ ___n

7. s___cc___ss · · · · · · 8. th___ ___ght

Topic 3

Choose the correct second syllable from the boxes to complete each word.

| bish | ror | nis | tle |

9. bat_____

10. rub_____

11. ter_____

12. ten_____

Topic 4

Indicate whether the verbs in these sentences are in the present (Pr), past (P) or future (F) tense.

13 The sun will shine tomorrow. (____)

14 Dan baked a cake last week. (____)

15 I am too cold. (____)

16 My friends will soon be here. (____)

Topic 5

Choose the correct prefix to begin each word.

super	sur	sub	semi

17 _____face

18 _____way

19 _____circle

20 _____market

Topic 6

Write the opposite of each adjective.

21 empty _____

22 narrow _____

23 tame _____

24 blunt _____

Mark the test. Remember to fill in your score on page 3.

Write your score out of 24.

Add a bonus point if you scored 20 or more.

TOTAL SCORE FOR TEST 1

Topic 7: Synonyms

Synonyms are words with the **same** or **similar** meanings.

conceal		hide

Practice

1 **Match up the pairs of synonyms.**

Write them here.

Use a thesaurus. Find one more synonym to go with each pair.

strike	start	_____	_____
hurry	broad	_____	_____
begin	hit	**strike hit**	**beat**
narrow	leave	_____	_____
wide	rush	_____	_____
go	thin	_____	_____
call	intelligent	_____	_____
clever	horrible	_____	_____
hard	shout	_____	_____
nasty	difficult	_____	_____

Challenge

2 Underline the word in each line that has a similar meaning to the word on the left in bold.

Use a thesaurus. Find a synonym to go with each pair.

a	**correct**	boastful sad	<u>right</u>	disgraceful	**accurate**
b	**adversity**	enemy misfortune building joy			
c	**despise**	clever scorn	sly	famous	
d	**hideous**	splendid ordinary	horrible	gorgeous	
e	**tranquil**	examine misfortune separate calm			
f	**sever**	hurry linger	separate	arrange	
g	**brink**	edge summit	slope	top	
h	**moist**	extreme damp	pure	vast	

3 Write down as many words as possible that have a similar meaning to the words below. Use a thesaurus to help you.

a	**say**	
b	**run**	
c	**nice**	
d	**big**	
e	**walk**	
f	**ask**	
g	**like**	
h	**touch**	

Topic 8: Parts of speech – adverbs

Get started

An **adverb** tells us more about a **verb**. It **adds meaning** to the verb.

Adverbs often tell us **how** something happened. Many adverbs end in **ly**.

Cara stroked the cat **gently**.

Practice

1 **Think of a suitable adverb ending in** ly **to complete each sentence.**

a I walked _____ to school because I was late.

b I dressed _____ to go to the party.

c The car braked _____ when the child ran into the road.

d I shouted _____ when I won the prize.

e The dog growled _____ at the stranger.

f We all laughed _____ at the joke.

g I stepped _____ on each stepping stone across the river.

h I cried _____ when my pet cat died.

i We listened _____ to our teacher's instructions.

j Last night it rained _____.

k Mr Hills waited _____ at the bus stop.

l The actors performed _____ in the play.

Challenge

2 **Circle the odd one out in each set of adverbs.**

a secretly	furtively	quietly	sneakily
b keenly	usually	eagerly	enthusiastically
c bravely	courageously	happily	valiantly
d carefully	warily	awkwardly	cautiously
e shyly	angrily	timidly	bashfully
f fairly	cunningly	slyly	craftily
g sadly	tiredly	wearily	exhaustedly
h foolishly	equally	stupidly	senselessly
i swiftly	quickly	speedily	pleasantly
j nervously	cleverly	worriedly	anxiously

3 **Rewrite the sentences.**
Change the adverb in each one to make it mean the opposite.

a I sighed happily. _____

b The children spoke noisily. _____

c I put my clothes tidily on the chair. _____

d I did all my sums incorrectly. _____

e The nurse treated me gently. _____

f The river flowed rapidly. _____

g The boy spoke politely. _____

h I did my writing carelessly. _____

i The thief answered honestly. _____

j The child spoke clearly. _____

Topic 9: Common sayings

Some common sayings have been around for **a long time**.

They are sometimes **hard to understand**!

It's raining cats and dogs.	←	This really means: It's raining hard!

Practice

1 **Match the beginnings and endings of these well-known sayings.**

Beginnings	Endings
The early bird	are soon parted.
New brooms	run deep.
A fool and his money	deserves another.
No news	catches the worm.
Practice	sweep clean.
Great minds	blames his tools.
Still waters	makes perfect.
A friend in need	keeps the doctor away.
One good turn	is a friend indeed.
Early to bed	is good news.
A bad workman	early to rise.
An apple a day	think alike.

Challenge

2 **Match up each saying with its correct meaning.**

to put the cart before the horse	to act unfairly
to sit on the fence	to overdo work and play
to hang your head	to refuse to take sides in an argument
to strike while the iron is hot	to be ashamed of yourself
to face the music	to do things the wrong way round
to hit below the belt	to be exactly right
to hit the nail on the head	to take punishment without complaint
to kick up a stink	to act while conditions are favourable
to hold one's tongue	to create a row
to burn the candle at both ends	to keep silent

3 **Say what you think we are meant to learn from these common sayings.**

a Don't put all your eggs in one basket.
b A rolling stone gathers no moss.
c One man's meat is another man's poison.
d Make hay while the sun shines.
e Empty vessels make most noise.
f Cut your coat according to your cloth.
g Birds of a feather flock together.
h Every cloud has a silver lining.
i Out of the frying pan into the fire.
j Don't count your chickens before they are hatched.

Topic 10: Parts of speech – pronouns

A **pronoun** is a word that **takes the place of a noun**.

Kiran got told off when **he** was late.

Pronouns may be either **singular** or **plural**.

A piece of writing may be written in:

the **1ˢᵗ person** when it is about **ourselves**, e.g. **I** (singular), **we** (plural)

the **2ⁿᵈ person** when it is about **you**, e.g. **you** (may be singular or plural)

the **3ʳᵈ person** when it is about **others**, e.g. **he, she, it** (singular), **they** (plural)

Practice

1 **Write** who **or** what **each underlined pronoun stands for.**

a Sophie has a cat. <u>She</u> (_____) is always stroking <u>it</u> (_____).

b Tom wanted the trainers but <u>they</u> (_____) were too dear for <u>him</u> (_____).

c "Are <u>you</u> (_____) ready?" Mrs Barnes asked the twins.

d When the baby saw Ben, <u>he</u> (_____) made <u>her</u> (_____) laugh.

e The children went to call for their friends but <u>they</u> (_____) were not in.

f "<u>I</u> (_____) love loud music," Jenny said.

Challenge

2 **Say in which person the underlined pronouns are written.**

a <u>I</u> read a book. (<u>**1ˢᵗ person singular**</u>)

b <u>He</u> rides a bike. (_____)

c <u>They</u> are happy. (_____)

d <u>She</u> has a bag. (_____)

e <u>It</u> is going fast. (_____)

f <u>We</u> are at home. (_____)

g "What are <u>you</u> doing?" the teacher asked Ben. (_____)

h "Where are <u>you</u> going?" the man asked the boys. (_____)

3 **Fill in the pronoun that has been missed out of each sentence.**

a Last night, _____ began to snow. (3ʳᵈ person singular)

b Will _____ pass me that newspaper, please? (2ⁿᵈ person singular)

c _____ love playing computer games. (1ˢᵗ person singular)

d Sam called for Emma and then _____ went to the park. (3ʳᵈ person plural)

e Anna is untidy. _____ leaves her clothes everywhere. (3ʳᵈ person singular)

f Ben put on his boots. _____ ran onto the football pitch. (3ʳᵈ person singular)

4 **This story is written in the 3ʳᵈ person. Underline all the pronouns in it.**

Sam did not like the woods at night. He could hear strange sounds all around. He decided to get out as quickly as possible. He began to run. Just then Sam heard an even louder noise. He stopped. He peered into the darkness but he could see nothing. Soon Sam was out of the woods. He was safe at last!

Topic 11: Suffixes

Get started

A **suffix** is a **group of letters** that is added to the **end** of a word.

A suffix may change the **job** the word does.

danger	dangerous
noun	adjective

Practice

1 **Make these nouns into adjectives ending in ous. Take care with the spelling!**

Set 1

noun	adjective
danger	dangerous
peril	
mountain	
poison	

Set 2

noun	adjective
fame	famous
nerve	
adventure	
ridicule	

Set 3

noun	adjective
mystery	mysterious
fury	
luxury	
glory	

2 **Complete each sentence, explaining what you noticed about each set.**

Set 1 The spelling of the noun remained the _____ when **ous** was added.

Set 2 In this set of words, the letter ____ at the end of the words was _____ before the suffix **ous** was added.

Set 3 In the words in this set, the letter _____ was changed to _____ before the suffix **ous** was added.

3 Underline the suffix in each adjective. Write the noun from which each adjective comes. Take care! The spelling of the noun will need altering a little.

adjective	noun
beauti<u>ful</u>	beauty
hungry	_____
responsible	_____
wondrous	_____
argumentative	_____
glorious	_____
circular	_____
fortunate	_____

adjective	noun
roguish	_____
awful	_____
Portuguese	_____
gigantic	_____
memorable	_____
metallic	_____
furry	_____
natural	_____

4 Add one of the suffixes in the box to each noun to change it into an adjective. Sometimes you may have to change the spelling of the noun slightly to do so.

ous	y	ic	ful	ive	ian	al

noun	adjective
nation	national
adventure	_____
water	_____
athlete	_____
force	_____
secret	_____
tragedy	_____
victory	_____

noun	adjective
smoke	_____
plenty	_____
centre	_____
Canada	_____
response	_____
fame	_____
poet	_____
Brazil	_____

Topic 12: Parts of speech – prepositions

Get started

A **preposition** is a word that shows the **relationship** of one thing to another. Prepositions often tell us about **position**.

There were lots of apples **on** the tree.

Practice

1 Here are some common prepositions.

above	across	behind	below	between	down
from	near	over	through	under	

Write the prepositions with:

four letters	__ __ __ __ __ __ __ __ __ __ __ __ __ __ __ __
five letters	__ __ __ __ __ __ __ __ __ __ __ __ __ __ __
six letters	__ __ __ __ __ __ __ __ __ __ __ __
seven letters	__ __ __ __ __ __ __ __ __ __ __ __ __ __

2 Fill in the missing vowels in these prepositions.

a __ b __ v __   **b** __ cr __ ss   **c** b __ h __ nd   **d** b __ l __ w

e b __ tw __ __ n   **f** d __ wn   **g** fr __ m   **h** n __ __ r

i __ v __ r   **j** thr __ __ gh   **k** __ nd __ r   **l** __ p __ n

Challenge

3 Match up the pairs of prepositions with opposite meanings.

on	under
above	without
over	before
down	off
inside	to
with	below
from	up
after	outside

4 Find and underline a preposition in each of these words.

a thunder

b supplier

c rainbow

d office

e hovered

f pond

g Dover

h rafters

5 Think of a suitable preposition to complete each of the following phrases.

a according _____

b conflict _____

c to be good _____

d to apply _____

e to be angry _____

f to get the blame _____

g to shrink _____

h to be ashamed _____

i to aim _____

j to despair _____

k in defiance _____

l to be disgusted _____

m to be conscious _____

n to have a dislike _____

o to fill _____

p to wait _____

q to write _____

r to suffer _____

s to meddle _____

t opposite _____

u guilty _____

Test 2 (Score 1 mark for every correct answer.)

Topic 7

1–4 Match up the words in Set A to the words in Set B with similar meanings.

Set A	clever	peaceful	strike	commence

Set B	calm	intelligent	start	hit

Topic 8

Match up the adverbs with opposite meanings.

5 gently   rudely

6 rapidly   roughly

7 politely   sadly

8 merrily   slowly

Topic 9

Choose the correct word from the box to complete each well-known saying.

bird	vessels	broom	minds

9 Empty _____ make most noise.

10 Great _____ think alike.

11 The early _____ catches the worm.

12 A new _____ sweeps clean.

Topic 10

Say who **or** what **each underlined pronoun stands for.**

13 "What are <u>you</u> (_____) doing?" the teacher asked Ben.

14 The wind blew so hard <u>it</u> (_____) blew a tree down.

15 "<u>We</u> (_____) love singing," the twins said.

16 Sam called for Emma and Amy but <u>they</u> (_____) weren't in.

Topic 11

Add the suffixes to the nouns to make some adjectives.

Spell the words you make correctly.

17 beauty + ful = _____   **18** adventure + ous = _____

19 response + ible = _____   **20** fortune + ate = _____

Topic 12

Fill in the missing vowels to make some prepositions.

21 ___b___v___   **22** ___ ___ts___d___

23 ___v___r   **24** b___n___ ___th

Mark the test. Remember to fill in your score on page 3.

Write your score out of 24.

Add a bonus point if you scored 20 or more.

TOTAL SCORE FOR TEST 2

Get started

English is **not** just **one language**. Over the years, we have incorporated words from many other languages.

Ballet is really a French word.

Practice

We have 'borrowed' all these et **words from French.**

duvet	trumpet	banquet	sachet	ballet
scarlet	bracket	bouquet	cabaret	blanket

1 Use the words to complete this chart.

et sounds like ay in day	et sounds like et in wet

2 Now use the words to complete these sentences.

a A ____duvet____ is a bed covering.   b _____ is a bright red colour.

c A _____ is a bunch of flowers.   d _____ is a type of dance.

e A _____ is a small packet.   f A _____ holds up a shelf.

g A _____ is a brass instrument.   h A _____ is a special feast.

i A _____ goes over a sheet.   j A _____ is a variety of different entertainments.

Challenge

3 Below are some Italian and Spanish words we have 'borrowed'. The Italian words are all to do with music and the arts. The Spanish words are all to do with activities of old Spanish explorers. Sort the words into sets.

piano	chocolate
ballerina	violin
galleon	banana
soprano	opera
tomato	hurricane
potato	concert

words from Italian	words from Spanish

4 These words come from India. Write what each word means.

pyjamas _____

verandah _____

shampoo _____

bungalow _____

5 A lot of our words originate from Greek. Write one of the English words you think we get from each Greek root word.

biology
dialogue
grammar
optician
astrology
television
metre
cosmetic
microphone
politics
sphere
pathetic

Greek root word	meaning	English word
aster	star	
bios	life	
kosmos	beauty	
logos	word/speech	
metron	a measure	
pathos	suffering	
phone	sound	
polis	city	
gramma	letter/thing written	
tele	from afar	
sphaira	globe/ball	
optikus	to do with sight	

Topic 14: Word order

Sometimes we can **change the order of words** within a sentence **without changing the meaning** of the sentence.

Last week I caught a cold.   I caught a cold last week.

Practice

1 **Underline the adverb in each sentence. Rewrite each sentence, beginning with the adverb.**

a The old car rattled <u>noisily</u> along the street.
  Noisily, the old car rattled along the street.

b Anna quickly did her homework.

c The thief crept quietly around the house.

d Sam dribbled past his opponent skilfully.

e The wind got up suddenly.

f I did my best writing neatly.

g Tom smiled at his old aunt sweetly.

h The carthorse plodded tiredly up the hill.

i I gasped breathlessly, "I can't go on!"

j Tara accepted the winning cup graciously.

Challenge

2 **Underline the conjunction in each sentence. Rewrite each sentence, beginning with the conjunction.**

a We will go out <u>if</u> the weather is fine.

If the weather is fine, we will go out.

b Jack read a book while I ate my tea.

_____

c Mum is not happy unless we are good.

_____

d The crowd cheered as the band played.

_____

e We can go out when our uncle arrives.

_____

f I would buy a car if I won a lot of money.

_____

g The bell rang while I was in the bath.

_____

h You can't see unless you open your eyes!

_____

3 **Find a way of rearranging the words in each sentence without altering its meaning.**

a We went to France on holiday. _____

b Tom had a drink when he stopped. _____

c The owl hunted for prey at night. _____

d The car stopped suddenly. _____

e The girl looked shyly at the boy. _____

f The woman laughed as she came in. _____

g The bear appeared out of the woods. _____

h A child sat under the old oak tree. _____

i Shut the door, please. _____

j There were six apples in the bag. _____

Get started

It was a rel**ie**f when the th**ie**f who robbed my n**ie**ce rec**ei**ved a long jail sentence.

A **useful** spelling **rule** for this **ee** sound is: **i** comes **before e** but **not after c**.

Practice

1 **Make these words:**

a

ie

th**ie**f   f____ld   sh____ld   p____ce   n____ce

_____thief_____   _____   _____   _____   _____

b

ie

br____f   f____rce   p____rce   ach____ve   bel____ve

_____   _____   _____   _____   _____

2 **Choose ie or ei to complete each word. Remember the rule!**

a shr**ie**k	b rec____ve	c pr____st	d c____ling	e misch____f
___shriek___	_____	_____	_____	_____
f p____ce	g dec____ve	h sh____ld	i rel____f	j conc____t
_____	_____	_____	_____	_____
k y____ld	l bel____ve	m rec____pt	n gr____f	o perc____ve
_____	_____	_____	_____	_____

Challenge

Here's another useful rule to remember:

> When adding a suffix beginning with **a** or **o** after a 'soft' **c** or **g**, always retain the silent **e** to keep the **c** or **g** 'soft'
> e.g. notice – noticeable; outrage – outrageous.

3 There are six mistakes in the words below. Follow the rule above.

Mark the spellings with a tick or cross and correct any mistakes.

a traceable ☐   b noticable ☐   c changable ☐   d manageable ☐

e couragous ☐   f advantagous ☐   g peaceable ☐   h serviceable ☐

i chargeable ☐   j enforcable ☐   k replaceable ☐   l outragous ☐

4 Complete the table of rules to help you remember about silent letters.

Use a dictionary and add more examples for each rule.

silent letter	rule	examples
b	often preceded by **m** at the end of words	com**b**
b	sometimes followed by **t**	dou**b**t
c	often preceded by **s**	s**c**issors
g	often followed by **n**	**g**nat
h	sometimes preceded by **g** or **r**	**g**hastly, r**h**yme
h	sometimes **h** comes at the beginning of a word and is followed by **o**	**h**onest
k	often followed by **n**	**k**now
l	often followed by **k** or **m**	fo**l**k, pa**l**m
n	usually preceded by **m**	colum**n**
p	often followed by **n** or **s**	**p**neumonia, **p**salm
t	often preceded by **s**	whis**t**le

Topic 16: Active and passive verbs

The girl **slammed** the door.	The door **was slammed** by the girl.
A verb is **active** when the **subject** of the sentence **performs the action**.	A verb is **passive** when the **subject** of the sentence has the **action done to it**.

Practice

1 Underline verbs in these sentences and indicate whether they are active (A) or passive (P).

a The snooker player <u>hit</u> the ball with his cue. (**A**)

b The people were rescued by the helicopter. (___)

c The treasure was buried by the pirates. (___)

d The flash of lightning illuminated the night sky. (___)

e The car was driven by a young man. (___)

f The monkey jumped from the tree. (___)

g Some foxes lived in the nearby wood. (___)

h The teacher read a story to the class. (___)

i The field was ploughed by the farmer. (___)

j The pilot landed the aeroplane safely on the runway. (___)

k The wedding dress was worn by the young bride. (___)

l I spent a lot of money on sweets. (___)

2 **Complete the passive verb in each sentence in a suitable way.**

a The car was _____ too fast by the foolish motorist.

b The ball was _____ hard by the tennis player.

c The cup was _____ convincingly by the school team.

d The precious jewels were _____ by a thief.

e The cake was _____ by Amy.

f The telephone was _____ by the butler.

g Many books were _____ by Roald Dahl.

h A new song was _____ by the pop singer.

i The baggy trousers were _____ by the funny clown.

j The diver was _____ by a man-eating shark.

3 **Underline the passive verbs in these sentences.**

Rewrite each sentence and change the verb from the passive to the active form.

a The cases were carried by the porter. **The porter carried the cases.**

b Some seeds were planted by the man. _____

c The tall beanstalk was grown by Jack. _____

d Guitars are played by some pop stars. _____

e The meal was served by the waiter. _____

f The car was driven by Dr Hill. _____

g Mountains are climbed by mountaineers. _____

h A mouse was caught by the owl. _____

i Some bread rolls were made by the baker. _____

j Tom was looked after by the nurse. _____

Get started

win	wine

Sometimes a **vowel** may have a **short** sound. Sometimes the same vowel may have a **long** sound.

watch

Sometimes vowels **don't sound how we expect them to!**

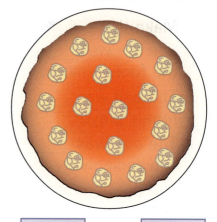

handle	pizza

The most **common** vowel at the **end of a word** is **e**. **Other vowels** are **less common**.

Practice

1 Add an e to the end of each word. Write the new word you make.

Say both words. Notice how the addition of the magic e **changes the sound of the vowel in the middle of the word.**

a fat ___**fate**___   b mop _____   c cub _____

d dam _____   e plum _____   f can _____

g hat _____   h hid _____   i kit _____

j din _____   k us _____   l shin _____

m slim _____   n cut _____   o strip _____

p rob _____   q not _____   r cod _____

s tub _____   t hop _____   u win _____

Challenge

2 **Make these words. In them the o sounds like u!**

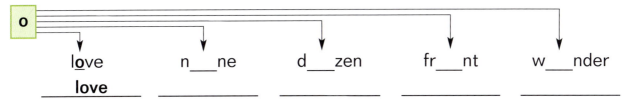

o

love   n___ne   d___zen   fr___nt   w___nder

__love__   _____   _____   _____   _____

3 **Make these words. In them the a sounds like o!**

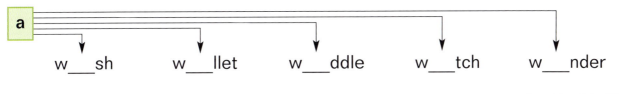

a

w___sh   w___llet   w___ddle   w___tch   w___nder

_____   _____   _____   _____   _____

4 **Make these words. In them the i sounds like a long e!**

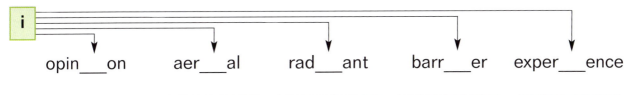

i

opin___on   aer___al   rad___ant   barr___er   exper___ence

_____   _____   _____   _____   _____

5 **The nouns in the word box end with a vowel other than e. To make the plural of most nouns ending with the vowels a, i, o or u, we just add s e.g. ski – skis.**

armadillo	banana	banjo	bongo	camera	cello	chapatti	cuckoo	dingo	emu
fiesta	gecko	igloo	kangaroo	kiwi	kimono	matzo	pasta	piano	piccolo
pizza	radio	risotto	samba	samosa	sauna	ski	sofa	tarantula	yoyo

Write the plural of each noun in the chart. Use a dictionary if necessary.

animal words	food words	music words	other words

Topic 18: Standard English

Get started

Standard English is the kind of language you are expected to use in school.

Me and Sam was soaking. ☒

Sam and I were soaking. ☑

Practice

1 Choose the correct form of the verb to complete each sentence.

a The bees _____ (was/were) buzzing round the flowers.

b What _____ (were/was) you doing last night?

c We _____ (was/were) late for school.

d Once upon a time there _____ (was/were) an ugly troll.

e Tom _____ (bringed/brought) his new bike to my house.

f I _____ (did/done) my homework quickly so I could go out.

g They _____ (has/have) some good teachers at our school.

h My mum _____ (give/gave) me a job to earn some money.

i I _____ (see/saw) a very boring film at the weekend.

j My friend _____ (don't/doesn't) like me any more.

k I _____ (wish/wishes) I could go to Spain on holiday.

l Sam _____ (run/ran) fast when the bull chased him.

Challenge

2 **Rewrite each sentence in Standard English. Avoid the use of double negatives.**

a There isn't no point in trying.   _____

b I don't want no sprouts.   _____

c I wasn't nowhere near him.   _____

d I don't read no books.   _____

e The girl didn't do nothing.   _____

f I never did nothing wrong.   _____

g The man never knew nobody.   _____

h I haven't won no prizes.   _____

i The boy hasn't been nowhere.   _____

j I didn't eat nothing nice.   _____

3 **Rewrite each sentence in Standard English.**

a Last week me and Tom watches telly.   _____

b Who's got me comic?   _____

c They'se goin' out soon.   _____

d I could of done it easy.   _____

e I ain't eatin' nothing.   _____

f What you starin' at?   _____

g We was just leaving.   _____

h Here's the magazine what I bought.   _____

i We done it yesterday.   _____

j That's real nice of you.   _____

Test 3 (Score 1 mark for every correct answer.)

The four words below came into our language from French.

Match up each word with its meaning.

1 | silhouette | someone paid to drive a car |

2 | souvenir | like a dark shadow |

3 | chauffeur | a counter where you can get refreshments |

4 | buffet | a keepsake |

Topic 14

Rewrite each sentence. Begin the sentence with the adverb.

5 The old car rattled slowly along. _____

6 The door suddenly opened. _____

7 The children came in noisily. _____

8 The old woman sat down wearily. _____

Topic 15

Choose ie or ei to complete each word.

9 sh____ld

10 rec____ve

11 c____ling

12 bel____ve

Topic 16

Indicate whether the verb in each sentence is active (A) or passive (P).

13 The grass was cut by Mr Barton.   (_____)

14 Mrs Hill made a cup of coffee.   (_____)

15 The helicopter was flown by a young pilot.   (_____)

16 I caught a bad cold last week.   (_____)

Topic 17

Choose a, i or o to complete each word.

17 w_____llet

18 fr_____nt

19 opin_____on

20 sw_____rm

Topic 18

Write each sentence correctly in Standard English.

21 They was playing football.   _____

22 He don't like me.   _____

23 I never did nothing wrong.   _____

24 Me and Ben went out.   _____

Mark the test. Remember to fill in your score on page 3.

Write your score out of 24.

Add a bonus point if you scored 20 or more.

TOTAL SCORE FOR TEST 3

Topic 19: Some tricky spellings

Get started

Always be on the lookout for tricky spellings!

For example, did you know that when **ar** comes after **w** it is often pronounced **or**, but when **or** comes after **w** it is often pronounced **er**?

a w**ar**m w**or**m

Practice

1 **Complete each word with** ar **or** or.

| w**or**m | w____m | w____ld | rew____d | sw____m |
| w____se | w____k | dw____ves | w____rant | w____th |

2 **Use the words you made to complete these sentences.**

a Snow White met seven _____.

b A _____ lives underground.

c It is important always to _____ hard.

d The _____ on which we live is part of a galaxy.

e I like _____ weather better than the cold.

f Two fifties are _____ a hundred.

g A _____ of angry wasps chased me.

h My writing is getting _____ rather than better!

i The police issued a _____ for the thief's arrest.

j Sam got a _____ for helping to catch the thief.

3 Complete each word with ch.

___ips	___estnut	___aracter	___ocolate	bro___ure
para___ute	___auffeur	___orus	stoma___	___oir
ben___	ma___ine	___ase	s___edule	a___e
___emist	___ampagne	laun___	___ef	e___o

4 Write each word in the chart.

ch (sounds like 'achoo')	ch (sounds like ck)	ch (sounds like sh)
chips	chemist	machine

5 Complete these words with cial, cious or cian.

a musi**cian**
  musician

b offi_____

c gra_____

d deli_____

e politi_____

f suspi_____

g spe_____

h electri_____

i so_____

6 What do you notice about the sound of ci in the words in question 5?

7 Complete these words with tial or tious.

a essen_____

b infec_____

c confiden_____

d ambi_____

e cau_____

f ini_____

8 What do you notice about the sound of ti in the words in question 7?

Topic 20: Clauses

Get started

A **clause** is a **group of words** which may be used as a **whole sentence**, or as **part of a sentence**. A clause usually contains a **subject** and a **verb**.

subject verb

The ugly troll lived in a dark cave.

This is a **one-clause** sentence.

Practice

1. Underline the subject and circle the verb in each of these one-clause sentences.

a The gardener mowed the grass.

b Most wolves hunt in packs.

c Some sheep were grazing in the field.

d A green alien emerged from the spacecraft.

e Dan drank a large bottle of fizzy lemonade.

f Whales swim under the water most of the time.

g Pandas eat bamboo shoots as their staple diet.

h We found an old suit of armour in the castle.

i Owls have good eyesight.

j The naughty toddler stamped his foot angrily.

k Some birds migrate to warmer countries in winter.

l The fearsome-looking giant grabbed Jack by the arm.

Challenge

2 **Choose the best subject from the box to complete each one-clause sentence.**

Underline the verb in each sentence to make sure there is only one!

The tree	We	A ship	The referee	Tailors
The ice	The wizard	Ben Nevis	Birds	The optician

a _____ blew the whistle.

b _____ cast a magic spell.

c _____ eat worms.

d _____ made the road slippery.

e _____ is a Scottish mountain.

f _____ make clothes.

g _____ hit the reef in the storm.

h _____ lost its leaves in winter.

i _____ get wool from sheep.

j _____ tested my eyes.

3 **Think of a suitable verb to complete each one-clause sentence.**

Underline the subject in each sentence.

a Foxes _____ in the woods.

b The farmer _____ his field.

c The stars _____ brightly at night.

d Some birds _____ nests in trees.

e Many cars _____ unleaded petrol.

f An aeroplane _____ on the runway.

g Thousands _____ the big match.

h French people _____ on the right.

i Tarantulas _____ huge and hairy.

j Tortoises _____ in winter.

k Trains _____ on rail lines.

l A ferry _____ across the Channel.

m Sam _____ the window.

n Athletes _____ races.

Topic 21: Mnemonics

Get started

A **mnemonic** is a **memory aid**.

We can use mnemonics to help us remember **tricky spellings**.

An island **is land** surrounded by water.

Practice

1 Underline the small word 'hiding' inside each longer word in the word wall.

	believe	great	separate	
young	bicycle	piece	busy	
	friend	ambitious	balloon	

2 Choose a word from above to complete each mnemonic.

a The **bus** was _____.	b Never _____ a **lie**.
c I would like a _____ of **pie**.	d A _____ looks like a **ball**.
e _____ has a **rat** in it.	f **You** are only _____ once.
g I will be your _____ until the very **end**.	h It's _____ to **eat**.
i I am not a **bit** _____.	j Don't ride a _____ in **icy** weather.

3 Choose a word from the box to complete each mnemonic.

fav**our**ite	w**eight**	**miser**able	con**science**	re**cog**nise
secretary	import**ant**	**govern**ment	**bread**th	cemetery

a What's the _____ of **eight** people?	**b** A **miser** is always _____.
c There's a **cog** in _____.	**d** The chief **ant** is the most _____.
e _____ is **our** best word.	**f** _____ has **science** in it.
g Three **e**'s are buried in a _____.	**h** **Bread** has _____.
i My _____ can keep a **secret**.	**j** The _____ must **govern**.

4 Underline a small word inside each longer word. Use it in your own mnemonic to help you remember the longer word.

vegetable	
chocolate	
skeleton	
cupboard	
headache	
sword	
temperature	
juice	
mathematics	
parallel	
soldier	
weather	
marriage	

Topic 22: Compound sentences

Get started

Remember – A **clause** is a **group of words** which may be used as a **whole sentence**, or as **part of a sentence**. A clause usually contains a **subject** and a **verb**.

subject   verb

The squirrel climbed the tree.

This is a **one-clause** sentence.

A **compound sentence** is made of **more than one clause**.

I picked the litter up because it looked ugly.

     clause 1   clause 2

Practice

1 Underline the verbs in these sentences. Indicate the number of clauses in each sentence.

a The cork <u>floated</u> on the surface of the water.   (one)

b The dragon emerged from the cave.   (_____)

c The clouds parted and the sun shone through.   (_____)

d I ate my curry and rice hungrily.   (_____)

e The race began after a while.   (_____)

f Cats purr but dogs bark.   (_____)

g I ran to the shop before it closed.   (_____)

h The boy with the broken glasses answered correctly.   (_____)

i Tom tackled two boys before he scored the goal.   (_____)

j I hate weekends because they are so boring!   (_____)

k The crowd clapped when the singer came on stage.   (_____)

l My uncle who lives in America visited England last week.   (_____)

2 Match up the beginnings and endings of these compound sentences. Underline the verb in each clause.

The children <u>ran</u> fast	if you come with me.
This is the rose bush	how you can do it.
Mark sharpened his pencil	had a puncture.
The car that crashed	before he drew the picture.
I will go	because they <u>were</u> late.
The boy hurt himself	because I wanted some sweets.
I went to the shop	when he bumped his head.
I will tell you	that I planted.

3 Rewrite each of these compound sentences as two separate sentences containing one clause. (You may have to alter the wording slightly in some cases.) Circle the verbs in the sentences you write.

a Anna picked some flowers and gave them to her mum.
   Anna (picked) some flowers. She (gave) them to her mum.

b Tom is very tired because he ran a marathon race yesterday.

   _____

c It poured with rain so we got soaking wet.

   _____

d We went to the station and we caught the train.

   _____

e I got all my spellings right but Emma did badly in the test.

   _____

f I like swimming but I can't dive very well.

   _____

Topic 23: Connectives

Connectives are words or phrases that can join together ideas or sentences.

The burglar broke the window **so that** he could get in.

Sometimes a connective may come **at the beginning** of the sentence.

Unless you tidy your room, you won't get any pocket money.

Practice

1 **Choose the best connective to join the pairs of clauses together.**

a It was very cold _____ (since/so) it was a relief to reach home.

b It is hard to learn the violin _____ (if/unless) you are prepared to practise.

c I saved up _____ (so that/as) I could buy a TV.

d I always try to do my homework _____ (although/before) I watch TV.

e I like to wear my wellingtons _____ (and/whenever) it rains a lot.

f The baby didn't stop crying _____ (until/during) she had a drink.

g My toy has been broken _____ (since/when) I accidentally trod on it.

h I listened to the music _____ (although/while) it was terrible.

i I got out the mower _____ (if/because) the grass needed cutting.

j I cleaned my teeth _____ (while/before) I went to bed.

k I stayed awake _____ (so/as long as) I was able to.

l I like coffee _____ (whereas/because) I hate tea.

Challenge

2 **Underline the connectives in these sentences. Rewrite each sentence, beginning with the connective.**

a I enjoyed the party **even though** I didn't think I would.
Even though I didn't think I would, I enjoyed the party.

b Mrs Barnes hung out the washing after the washing machine had finished.

_____

c Mr Green hummed to himself while he was having a bath.

_____

d I will always be your friend as long as you want me to.

_____

e I love to visit museums whenever I have time.

_____

f You can't have any pudding because you didn't eat your cabbage.

_____

g Do you go swimming whenever you can?

_____

h We will buy some doughnuts if we have enough money.

_____

3 **Make up some two-clause sentences of your own. Use these connectives to join the clauses.**

because	although
wherever	until
whereas	in order to
as long as	unless
so that	nevertheless

_____

_____

_____

_____

_____

_____

_____

_____

_____

Topic 24: Playing about with words

Get started

Playing with words can help us **learn** more **about spelling**.

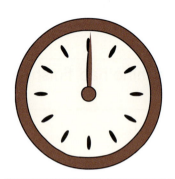

noon

A **palindrome** is a word that is spelt the **same backwards** or **forwards**.

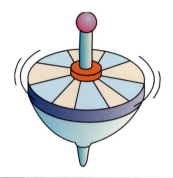

nips – spin

A **semordnilap** (palindromes backwards) can be spelt backwards to make **another** word.

care – race

An **anagram** mixes up the letters of a word to make another word.

Practice

1 Write each of these words backwards to make another word.

a star __**rats**__   b evil _____   c keep _____   d moor _____

e gulp _____   f part _____   g spot _____   h pans _____

i paws _____   j bats _____   k step _____   l reed _____

m pots _____   n now _____   o emit _____   p flog _____

2 Tick ☑ which of these words are semordnilaps.

a dew ☐   b taste ☐   c dark ☐   d gas ☐   e liar ☐

f moon ☐   g loop ☐   h into ☐   i pine ☐   j net ☐

k flow ☐   l paper ☐   m pens ☐   n devil ☐   o brag ☐

p hand ☐   q was ☐   r foot ☐   s tub ☐   t fuel ☐

Challenge

3 Indicate whether each word is a semordnilap (S) or a palindrome (P).

a civic (____)   b are (____)   c mum (____)   d level (____)

e mug (____)   f net (____)   g solos (____)   h doom (____)

i radar (____)   j nap (____)   k noon (____)   l madam (____)

m moor (____)   n eye (____)   o evil (____)   p deed (____)

q reed (____)   r peep (____)   s eve (____)   t rotor (____)

4 Work out the following anagrams.

word	anagram	word	anagram
mace	came	miles	
aids		asleep	
ales		stale	
art		earth	
rife		risen	
cafe		snap	
deal		warder	
lamp		peach	
scare		drop	
bore		state	
clean		wasp	
design		priest	
plane		prides	
stare		oils	

Test 4 (Score 1 mark for every correct answer.)

Topic 19

Complete each word with ar or or.

1 w____ld

2 w____th

3 w____der

4 w____ts

Topic 20

Underline the subject and circle the verb in each one-clause sentence.

5 The boy climbed the tree.

6 My cat likes cream.

7 Carpenters make things from wood.

8 Mr Douglas closed the door.

Topic 21

Find and underline a small word 'hiding' inside each of these tricky words.

9 friend

10 piece

11 great

12 young

Topic 22

Indicate whether each sentence contains one or two clauses.

13 I switched on the light.   (_____)

14 I undressed before I got into bed.   (_____)

15 I like sprouts but I hate cabbage!   (_____)

16 The crowd cheered wildly.   (_____)

Topic 23

Choose the best connective to complete each sentence.

17 It was hot _____ (since/so) I took off my coat.

18 You can't have a cake _____ (if/unless) you buy it yourself.

19 We didn't reach home _____ (until/during) it was midnight.

20 I finished my book _____ (while/before) I turned out the light.

Topic 24

21–**24** Match up the anagrams in Set A and Set B.

Set A	deal	warder	slate	blame

Set B	reward	amble	lead	steal

Mark the test. Now add up all your test scores and put your final score on page 3.

Write your score out of 24.   [   ]

Add a bonus point if you scored 20 or more.   [   ]

TOTAL SCORE FOR TEST 4   [   ]

Answers

Topic 1: Common letter strings (page 4)

1.

a. illustrate; educate; chocolate; separate; deliberate; considerate
b. athlete; compete; complete; delete; concrete; obsolete
c. definite; favourite; dynamite; opposite; polite; recite

2.

fragrant/arrogant
badge/hedgehog
crouch/touch
factory/story
disturb/burgle
fruit/bruise
plaque/antique
beaten/sweaty
tongue/catalogue
warehouse/scared

3.

The correct letter strings are underlined. The words used are examples only (other answers are possible).
Left-hand column: sector; adventure; slice; generous; taught; vegetarian; sheer
Right-hand column: sugar; cough; carnival; unless; tolerance; flavour; pinnacle

Topic 2: Parts of speech – nouns (page 6)

1.

names of people	names of places	names of things
doctor	dock	orange
astronaut	hangar	moon
dentist	bank	lorry
carpenter	library	cup
plumber	church	pencil
editor	stadium	computer
	factory	leaf

2.

a. Mount Kilimanjaro is the highest mountain in Africa.
b. Edinburgh is the capital city of Scotland.
c. I bought a copy of the Daily Mirror and the TV Times.
d. Yesterday was Thursday, the first day of December.
e. Sir Francis Drake was a sailor in the reign of Queen Elizabeth the First.
f. We went to the Gaumont Cinema in Luton.

3.

a. strength **b.** courage **c.** poverty **d.** fear **e.** speed **f.** belief

Topic 3: Double letters (page 8)

1.

root word	+ suffix **er**	+ suffix **est**	+ suffix **ing**	+ suffix **ed**
hop	hopper	—	hopping	hopped
skip	skipper	—	skipping	skipped
bat	batter	—	batting	batted
hum	hummer	—	humming	hummed
sad	sadder	saddest	—	—
fit	fitter	fittest	fitting	fitted
plan	planner	—	planning	planned
jog	jogger	—	jogging	jogged
hot	hotter	hottest	—	—
flat	flatter	flattest	—	—
big	bigger	biggest	—	—
ban	banner	—	banning	banned
but	butter	—	butting	butted
wet	wetter	wettest	wetting	wetted

2.

a. terror	**b.** arrive	**c.** banner	**d.** barrow	**e.** dinner
f. ribbon	**g.** lesson	**h.** message	**i.** flurry	**j.** carry
k. common	**l.** marriage	**m.** summer	**n.** rummage	**o.** rabbit
p. borrow	**q.** hammer	**r.** burrow	**s.** carriage	**t.** horror

3.

a. ter/ror	**b.** ar/rive	**c.** ban/ner	**d.** bar/row	**e.** din/ner
f. rib/bon	**g.** les/son	**h.** mes/sage	**i.** flur/ry	**j.** car/ry
k. com/mon	**l.** mar/riage	**m.** sum/mer	**n.** rum/mage	**o.** rab/bit
p. bor/row	**q.** ham/mer	**r.** bur/row	**s.** car/riage	**t.** hor/ror

4.

a. ✓	**b.** ✗ omitting	**c.** ✗ marvellous	**d.** ✓
e. ✓	**f.** ✗ deterrent	**g.** ✗ rebellion	**h.** ✓
i. ✓	**j.** ✗ traveller	**k.** ✓	**l.** ✗ forgotten
m. ✗ permitting	**n.** ✓	**o.** ✗ metallic	**p.** ✓
q. ✓	**r.** ✗ incurring	**s.** ✓	**t.** ✗ levelled

Topic 4: Parts of speech – verbs (page 10)

1.

a. Pr **b.** P **c.** F **d.** Pr **e.** P **f.** F **g.** Pr **h.** P **i.** F **j.** Pr **k.** P
l. F **m.** Pr **n.** P **o.** F **p.** Pr

2.

a. is/Pr **b.** was/P **c.** am/Pr **d.** were/P **e.** will/F **f.** have/P
g. has/P **h.** will/F **i.** is/Pr **j.** was/P **k.** is/Pr **l.** was/P
m. am/Pr **n.** were/P **o.** will/F **p.** have/P

3.

a. If you are tired you ^should^ go to bed.
b. I ^would^ buy the video game if I had enough money.
c. I ^could/would^ cross the road if it wasn't so busy.
d. I told you that if you practised you ^would^ get better.
e. If horses had wings they ^could/would^ fly!
f. You ^should^ not stay out in direct sunshine too long.
g. I ^could or would^ not eat my dinner because it was cold.
h. I ^would^ be grateful if you help me.
i. If I buy a ticket I ^might^ win.
j. If it rains tomorrow, I ^might^ get wet.

Topic 5: Prefixes (page 12)

1.

a. automobile	**b.** bilingual	**c.** disagree	**d.** extraordinary
e. illegal	**f.** interview	**g.** microscope	**h.** aquaplane
i. submarine	**j.** superhuman	**k.** prehistoric	**l.** centimetre
m. disappear	**n.** bicycle	**o.** surplus	**p.** inland
q. semicircle	**r.** outdo	**s.** unwell	**t.** export

2.

Definitions: not secure, a three-sided shape, half a circle, something that doesn't make sense, a message added to a letter as an afterthought, behave badly, play again, the distance around something, current beneath the surface, draw back, equal-sided

3.

Many answers are possible for the middle column of the table.
Meanings: against, air, earth, from afar, over or beyond, alone or single, independently, many, small, one, between or among, out of, in front of

Topic 6: **Parts of speech – adjectives** (page 14)

1.

a. sunny/hot
b. huge/thrilling
c. hungry/tired/thirsty
d. old/little/thatched
e. ancient/bony
f. magnificent/beautiful
g. first/brilliant/red
h. shaggy/black/juicy
i. rough/woollen
j. weary/disheartened
k. strange/metallic

2.

adjectives to do with:			
colour	size	feelings	taste
red	huge	scared	sweet
brown	thin	amazed	salty
yellow	short	bored	spicy
silver	tall	happy	sour

3 and 4.
Personal answers.

Test 1 (page 16)

Topic 1	**1.** tory	**2.** que	**3.** ar	**4.** ice
Topic 2	**5.** knowledge	**6.** expectation	**7.** success	**8.** thought
Topic 3	**9.** battle	**10.** rubbish	**11.** terror	**12.** tennis
Topic 4	**13.** F	**14.** P	**15.** Pr	**16.** F
Topic 5	**17.** surface	**18.** subway	**19.** semicircle	**20.** supermarket
Topic 6	Other answers are possible.			
	21. full	**22.** wide	**23.** wild	**24.** sharp

Topic 7: **Synonyms** (page 18)

1.
The third synonyms (in brackets below) are examples only.
begin/start/(commence)
narrow/thin/(slim)
wide/broad/(extensive)
clever/intelligent/(smart)
strike/hit/(beat)
nasty/horrible/(unpleasant)
go/leave/(depart)
call/shout/(yell)
hurry/rush/(dash)
hard/difficult/(demanding)

2.
The third synonyms (in brackets below) are examples only.
a. right/(accurate) **b.** misfortune/ (disaster)
c. scorn/(dislike) **d.** horrible/(ugly)
e. calm/(peaceful) **f.** separate/ (break)
g. edge/(limit) **h.** damp/(wet)

3.
Personal answers.

Topic 8: **Parts of speech – adverbs** (page 20)

1.
Examples only (many answers are possible):
a. quickly
b. fashionably
c. suddenly
d. happily
e. loudly
f. merrily
g. carefully
h. unhappily
i. quietly
j. heavily
k. patiently
l. brilliantly

2.
a. quietly
b. usually
c. happily
d. awkwardly
e. angrily
f. fairly
g. sadly
h. equally
i. pleasantly
j. cleverly

3.
For example:
a. I sighed unhappily.
b. The children spoke quietly.
c. I put my clothes untidily on the chair.
d. I did all my sums correctly.
e. The nurse treated me roughly.
f. The river flowed slowly.
g. The boy spoke rudely.
h. I did my writing carefully.
i. The thief answered dishonestly.
j. The child spoke unclearly.

Topic 9: **Common sayings** (page 22)

1.
The early bird catches the worm. New brooms sweep clean. A fool and his money are soon parted. No news is good news. Practice makes perfect. Great minds think alike. Still waters run deep. A friend in need is a friend indeed. One good turn deserves another. Early to bed early to rise. A bad workman blames his tools. An apple a day keeps the doctor away.

2.
to put the cart before the horse – to do things the wrong way round; to sit on the fence – to refuse to take sides in an argument; to hang your head – to be ashamed of yourself; to strike while the iron is hot – to act while conditions are favourable; to face the music – to take punishment without complaint; to hit below the belt – to act unfairly; to hit the nail on the head – to be exactly right; to kick up a stink – to create a row; to hold one's tongue – to keep silent; to burn the candle at both ends – to overdo work and play

3.
Suggested answers:
a. Leave your options open.
b. A person who keeps moving doesn't collect much or achieve much.
c. What one person loves another person will hate.
d. Do what you can while the conditions are good.
e. People who know the least, speak the most.
f. Don't overstretch yourself.
g. People associate with people who are similar to them.
h. There is something good in every bad situation.
i. From one problem to a worse problem.
j. Don't assume anything before it has happened.

Topic 10: **Parts of speech – pronouns** (page 24)

1.
a. Sophie/the cat
b. the trainers/Tom
c. the twins
d. Ben/the baby
e. their friends
f. Jenny

2.
a. 1st person singular
b. 3rd person singular
c. 3rd person plural
d. 3rd person singular
e. 3rd person singular
f. 1st person plural
g. 2nd person singular
h. 2nd person plural

3.
a. it
b. you
c. I
d. they
e. She
f. He

4.
Sam did not like the woods at night. He could hear strange sounds all around. He decided to get out as quickly as possible. He began to run. Just then Sam heard an even louder noise. He stopped. He peered into the darkness but he could see nothing. Soon Sam was out of the woods. He was safe at last!

Topic 11: **Suffixes** (page 26)

1.

Set 1: dangerous; perilous; mountainous; poisonous
Set 2: famous; nervous; adventurous; ridiculous
Set 3: mysterious; furious; luxurious; glorious

2.

Set 1: The spelling of the noun remained the **same** when **ous** was added.
Set 2: In this set of words, the letter **e** at the end of the words was **removed** before the suffix **ous** was added.
Set 3: In the words in this set, the letter **y** was changed to **i** before the suffix **ous** was added.

3.

beautiful – beauty;
hungry – hunger;
responsible – response;
wondrous – wonder;
argumentative – argument;
glorious – glory;
circular – circle;
fortunate – fortune;

roguish – rogue
awful – awe
Portuguese – Portugal
gigantic – giant
memorable – memory
metallic – metal
furry – fur
natural – nature

4.

nation – national;
adventure – adventurous;
water – watery;
athlete – athletic;
force – forceful;
secret – secretive;
tragedy – tragic;
victory – victorious;

smoke – smoky
plenty – plentiful
centre – central
Canada – Canadian
response – responsive
fame – famous
poet – poetic
Brazil – Brazilian

Topic 12: **Parts of speech – prepositions** (page 28)

1.

four letters:	down	from	near	over
five letters:	above	below	under
six letters:	across	behind
seven letters:	between	through

2.

a. above	**b.** across	**c.** behind	**d.** below	**e.** between	**f.** down
g. from	**h.** near	**i.** over	**j.** through	**k.** under	**l.** upon

3.

on/off; above/below; over/under; down/up; inside/outside; with/without; from/to; after/before

4.

a. thunder	**b.** supplier	**c.** rainbow	**d.** office
e. hovered	**f.** pond	**g.** Dover	**h.** rafters

5.

For example (other answers may be possible):

a. to	**b.** with	**c.** for	**d.** to	**e.** with	**f.** for	**g.** into
h. of	**i.** for	**j.** about	**k.** of	**l.** with	**m.** of	**n.** of
o. with	**p.** for	**q.** about	**r.** for	**s.** with	**t.** to	**u.** of

Test 2 (page 30)

Topic 7 1–4. clever/intelligent; peaceful/calm; strike/hit; commence/start

Topic 8	**5.** gently/ roughly	**6.** rapidly/ slowly	**7.** politely/ rudely	**8.** merrily/ sadly
Topic 9	**9.** vessels	**10.** minds	**11.** bird	**12.** broom
Topic 10	**13.** Ben	**14.** the wind	**15.** the twins	**16.** Emma and Amy
Topic 11	**17.** beautiful	**18.** adventurous	**19.** responsible	**20.** fortunate
Topic 12	**21.** above	**22.** outside	**23.** over	**24.** beneath

Topic 13: **Word origins** (page 32)

1.

et sounds like **ay** in **day**: duvet, sachet, ballet, bouquet, cabaret
et sounds like **et** in **wet**: trumpet, banquet, scarlet, bracket, blanket

2.

a. duvet	**b.** Scarlet	**c.** bouquet	**d.** Ballet	**e.** sachet
f. bracket	**g.** trumpet	**h.** banquet	**i.** blanket	**j.** cabaret

3.

words from Italian: piano, ballerina, opera, soprano, violin, concert
words from Spanish: tomato, banana, potato, galleon, chocolate, hurricane

4.

pyjamas – shirt and trousers to sleep in; verandah – an open porch; shampoo – something that cleans hair; bungalow – a house with only one storey

5.

English words: astrology; biology; cosmetic; dialogue; metre; pathetic; microphone; politics; grammar; television; sphere; optician

Topic 14: **Word order** (page 34)

1.

a. The old car rattled <u>noisily</u> along the street.	Noisily, the old car rattled along the street.
b. Anna <u>quickly</u> did her homework.	Quickly, Anna did her homework.
c. The thief crept <u>quietly</u> around the house.	Quietly, the thief crept around the house.
d. Sam dribbled past his opponent <u>skilfully</u>.	Skilfully, Sam dribbled past his opponent.
e. The wind got up <u>suddenly</u>.	Suddenly, the wind got up.
f. I did my best writing <u>neatly</u>.	Neatly, I did my best writing.
g. Tom smiled at his old aunt <u>sweetly</u>.	Sweetly, Tom smiled at his old aunt.
h. The carthorse plodded <u>tiredly</u> up the hill.	Tiredly, the carthorse plodded up the hill.
i. I gasped <u>breathlessly</u>, "I can't go on!"	Breathlessly, I gasped, "I can't go on!"
j. Tara accepted the winning cup <u>graciously</u>.	Graciously, Tara accepted the winning cup.

2.

a. We will go out <u>if</u> the weather is fine.	If the weather is fine, we will go out.
b. Jack read a book <u>while</u> I ate my tea.	While I ate my tea, Jack read a book.
c. Mum is not happy <u>unless</u> we are good.	Unless we are good, Mum is not happy.
d. The crowd cheered <u>as</u> the band played.	As the band played, the crowd cheered.
e. We can go out <u>when</u> our uncle arrives.	When our uncle arrives, we can go out.
f. I would buy a car <u>if</u> I won a lot of money.	If I won a lot of money, I would buy a car.
g. The bell rang <u>while</u> I was in the bath.	While I was in the bath, the bell rang.
h. You can't see <u>unless</u> you open your eyes!	Unless you open your eyes, you can't see!

3. Suggested answers.

a. We went on holiday to France.	**b.** When he stopped, Tom had a drink.
c. At night the owl hunted for prey.	**d.** Suddenly the car stopped.
e. Shyly, the girl looked at the boy.	**f.** As she came in, the woman laughed.
g. Out of the woods the bear appeared.	**h.** Under the old oak tree sat a child.
i. Please shut the door.	**j.** In the bag there were six apples.

Topic 15: **Spelling rules** (page 36)

1.

a. thief; field; shield; piece; niece	**b.** brief; fierce; pierce; achieve; believe

2.

a. shriek	**b.** receive	**c.** priest	**d.** ceiling	**e.** mischief
f. piece	**g.** deceive	**h.** shield	**i.** relief	**j.** conceit
k. yield	**l.** believe	**m.** receipt	**n.** grief	**o.** perceive

3.

a. ✓	**b.** ✗ noticeable	**c.** ✗ changeable	**d.** ✓
e. ✗ courageous	**f.** ✗ advantageous	**g.** ✓	**h.** ✓
i. ✓	**j.** ✗ enforceable	**k.** ✓	**l.** ✗ outrageous

4.

Personal answers.

Topic 16: **Active and passive verbs** (page 38)

1.

a. hit	(A)		**b.** were rescued	(P)
c. was buried	(P)		**d.** illuminated	(A)
e. was driven	(P)		**f.** jumped	(A)
g. lived	(A)		**h.** read	(A)
i. was ploughed	(P)		**j.** landed	(A)
k. was worn	(P)		**l.** spent	(A)

2.
For example (other answers may be possible):

a. driven **b.** hit **c.** won **d.** stolen **e.** baked
f. answered **g.** written **h.** recorded **i.** worn **j.** attacked

3.

a. were carried — The porter carried the cases.
b. were planted — The man planted some seeds.
c. was grown — Jack grew the tall beanstalk.
d. are played — Some pop stars play guitars.
e. was served — The waiter served the meal.
f. was driven — Dr Hill drove the car.
g. are climbed — Mountaineers climb mountains.
h. was caught — The owl caught a mouse.
i. were made — The baker made some bread rolls.
j. was looked — The nurse looked after Tom.

Topic 17: **Vowels** (page 40)

1.

a. fate **b.** mope **c.** cube **d.** dame **e.** plume **f.** cane **g.** hate
h. hide **i.** kite **j.** dine **k.** use **l.** shine **m.** slime **n.** cute
o. stripe **p.** robe **q.** note **r.** code **s.** tube **t.** hope **u.** wine

2.
love; none; dozen; front; wonder

3.
wash; wallet; waddle; watch; wander

4.
opinion; aerial; radiant; barrier; experience

5.

animal words	food words	music words	other words
armadillos	bananas	banjos	cameras
cuckoos	chapattis	bongos	igloos
dingos (**or** oes)	matzos	cellos	kimonos
emus	pastas	fiestas	saunas
geckos (**or** oes)	pizzas	pianos	skis
kangaroos	risottos	piccolos	sofas
kiwis	samosas	radios	yoyos
tarantulas		sambas	

Topic 18: **Standard English** (page 42)

1.

a. were **b.** were **c.** were **d.** was **e.** brought **f.** did
g. have **h.** gave **i.** saw **j.** doesn't **k.** wish **l.** ran

2. Other answers are possible.

a. There isn't any/is no point in trying. **b.** I don't want any sprouts.
c. I wasn't anywhere near him. **d.** I don't read any books.
e. The girl didn't do anything. **f.** I never did anything wrong.
g. The man never knew anybody. **h.** I haven't won any prizes.
i. The boy hasn't been anywhere. **j.** I didn't eat anything nice.

3. Suggested answers.

a. Last week Tom and I watched television. **b.** Who's got my comic?
c. They're going out soon. **d.** I could have done it easily.
e. I'm not eating anything. **f.** What are you staring at?
g. We were just leaving. **h.** Here's the magazine that I bought.
i. We did it yesterday. **j.** That's really nice of you.

Test 3 (page 44)

Topic 13
1. like a dark shadow
2. a keepsake
3. someone paid to drive a car
4. a counter where you can get refreshments

Topic 14
5. Slowly, the old car rattled along.
6. Suddenly, the door opened.
7. Noisily, the children came in.
8. Wearily, the old woman sat down.

Topic 15 **9.** shield **10.** receive **11.** ceiling **12.** believe
Topic 16 **13.** P **14.** A **15.** P **16.** A
Topic 17 **17.** wallet **18.** front **19.** opinion **20.** swarm

Topic 18 21. They were playing football. **22.** He doesn't like me.
23. I never did anything wrong. **24.** Ben and I went out.

Topic 19: **Some tricky spellings** (page 46)

1.

worm	warm	world	reward	swarm
worse	work	dwarves	warrant	worth

2.

a. dwarves **b.** worm **c.** work **d.** world **e.** warm
f. worth **g.** swarm **h.** worse **i.** warrant **j.** reward

3.

chips	chestnut	character	chocolate	brochure
parachute	chauffeur	chorus	stomach	choir
bench	machine	chase	schedule	ache
chemist	champagne	launch	chef	echo

4.

ch (sounds like 'achoo')	ch (sounds like **ck**)	ch (sounds like **sh**)
chips	character	brochure
chestnut	chorus	parachute
chocolate	stomach	chauffeur
bench	choir	machine
chase	ache	schedule
launch	chemist	champagne
	echo	chef

5.

a. musician **b.** official **c.** gracious
d. delicious **e.** politician **f.** suspicious
g. special **h.** electrician **i.** social

6.
In the words in question 5, the **ci** sounds like **sh**.

7.

a. essential **b.** infectious **c.** confidential
d. ambitious **e.** cautious **f.** initial

8.
In the words in question 7, the **ti** sounds like **sh**.

Topic 20: **Clauses** (page 48)

1.

a. The gardener (mowed) **b.** Most wolves (hunt)
c. Some sheep (were grazing) **d.** A green alien (emerged)
e. Dan (drank) **f.** Whales (swim)
g. Pandas (eat) **h.** We (found)
i. Owls (have) **j.** The naughty toddler (stamped)
k. Some birds (migrate) **l.** The fearsome-looking giant (grabbed)

2.

a. The referee/ **b.** The wizard/ **c.** Birds/<u>eat</u> **d.** The ice/ **e.** Ben Nevis/
<u>biew</u>   <u>cast</u>   <u>made</u>   <u>is</u>
f. Tailors/   **g.** A ship/<u>hit</u> **h.** The tree/ **i.** We/<u>get</u> **j.** The
<u>make</u>   <u>lost</u>   optician/
                                                                     <u>tested</u>

3.

The words in brackets are examples only.

a. <u>Foxes</u> (live) in the woods.   **b.** <u>The farmer</u> (ploughed) his field.
c. <u>The stars</u> (shine) brightly at night.   **d.** <u>Some birds</u> (build) nests in trees.
e. <u>Many cars</u> (use) unleaded petrol.   **f.** <u>An aeroplane</u> (landed) on the
                                                              runway.
g. <u>Thousands</u> (attended) the big match.   **h.** <u>French people</u> (drive) on the right.
i. <u>Tarantulas</u> (are) huge and hairy.   **j.** <u>Tortoises</u> (hibernate) in winter.
k. <u>Trains</u> (run) on rail lines.   **l.** <u>A ferry</u> (sailed) across the Channel.
m. <u>Sam</u> (opened) the window.   **n.** <u>Athletes</u> (run) races.

Topic 21: **Mnemonics** (page 50)

1.

beli<u>eve</u>		great		separ<u>ate</u> or separate	
<u>you</u>ng		bi<u>cycle</u> or bi<u>cycle</u>		piece		bu<u>sy</u> or b<u>usy</u>
fri<u>end</u>		am<u>bit</u>ious		ball<u>oon</u> or ball<u>oon</u>	

2.

a. busy **b.** believe **c.** piece **d.** balloon **e.** Separate
f. young **g.** friend **h.** great **i.** ambitious **j.** bicycle

3.

a. weight **b.** miserable **c.** recognise **d.** important **e.** Favourite
f. Conscience **g.** cemetery **h.** breadth **i.** secretary **j.** government

4.

Personal answers.

Topic 22: **Compound sentences** (page 52)

1.

a. The cork <u>floated</u> on the surface of the water.   (one)
b. The dragon <u>emerged</u> from the cave.   (one)
c. The clouds <u>parted</u> and the sun <u>shone</u> through.   (two)
d. I <u>ate</u> my curry and rice hungrily.   (one)
e. The race <u>began</u> after a while.   (one)
f. Cats <u>purr</u> but dogs <u>bark</u>.   (two)
g. I <u>ran</u> to the shop before it <u>closed</u>.   (two)
h. The boy with the broken glasses <u>answered</u> correctly.   (one)
i. Tom <u>tackled</u> two boys before he <u>scored</u> the goal.   (two)
j. I <u>hate</u> weekends because they <u>are</u> so boring!   (two)
k. The crowd <u>clapped</u> when the singer <u>came</u> on stage.   (two)
l. My uncle who <u>lives</u> in America <u>visited</u> England last week.   (two)

2.

The children <u>ran</u> fast because they <u>were</u> late.
This <u>is</u> the rose bush that I <u>planted</u>.
Mark <u>sharpened</u> his pencil before he <u>drew</u> the picture.
The car that <u>crashed</u> had a puncture.
I <u>will go</u> if you <u>come</u> with me.
The boy <u>hurt</u> himself when he <u>bumped</u> his head.
I <u>went</u> to the shop because I <u>wanted</u> some sweets.
I <u>will tell</u> you how you <u>can do</u> it.

3.

a. Anna (picked) some flowers. She (gave) them to her mum.
b. Tom (is) very tired. He (ran) a marathon race yesterday.
c. It (poured) with rain. We (got) soaking wet.
d. We (went) to the station. We (caught) the train.
e. I (got) all my spellings right. Emma (did) badly in the test.
f. I like swimming. I (can't dive) very well.

Topic 23: **Connectives** (page 54)

1.

a. so **b.** unless **c.** so that **d.** before **e.** whenever **f.** until
g. since **h.** although **i.** because **j.** before **k.** as long as **l.** whereas

2.

a. I enjoyed the party <u>even though</u> I didn't think I would.
Even though I didn't think I would, I enjoyed the party.
b. Mrs Barnes hung out the washing <u>after</u> the washing machine had finished.
After the washing machine had finished, Mrs Barnes hung out the washing.
c. Mr Green hummed to himself <u>while</u> he was having a bath.
While he was having a bath, Mr Green hummed to himself.
d. I will always be your friend <u>as long as</u> you want me to.
As long as you want me to, I will always be your friend.
e. I love to visit museums <u>whenever</u> I have time.
Whenever I have time, I love to visit museums.
f. You can't have any pudding <u>because</u> you didn't eat your cabbage.
Because you didn't eat your cabbage, you can't have any pudding.
g. Do you go swimming <u>whenever</u> you can?
Whenever you can, do you go swimming?
h. We will buy some doughnuts <u>if</u> we have enough money.
If we have enough money, we will buy some doughnuts.

3.

Personal answers.

Topic 24: **Playing about with words** (page 56)

1.

a. rats **b.** live **c.** peek **d.** room **e.** plug **f.** trap **g.** tops **h.** snap
i. swap **j.** stab **k.** pets **l.** deer **m.** stop **n.** won **o.** time **p.** golf

2.

a. ✓ **b.** ✗ **c.** ✗ **d.** ✓ **e.** ✓
f. ✗ **g.** ✓ **h.** ✗ **i.** ✗ **j.** ✓
k. ✓ **l.** ✗ **m.** ✗ **n.** ✓ **o.** ✓
p. ✗ **q.** ✓ **r.** ✗ **s.** ✓ **t.** ✗

3.

a. P **b.** S **c.** P **d.** P **e.** S
f. S **g.** P **h.** S **i.** P **j.** S
k. P **l.** P **m.** S **n.** P **o.** S
p. P **q.** S **r.** P **s.** P **t.** P

4.

Left-hand table: mace/came; aids/said; ales/sale; art/tar, rat; rife/fire; cafe/face; deal/lead, dale; lamp/palm; scare/cares, races, acres; bore/robe; clean/lance; design/signed; plane/panel; stare/rates
Right-hand table: miles/smile; asleep/please; stale/tales, slate, steal; earth/heart; risen/siren; snap/pans, naps, span; warder/drawer, redraw, reward; peach/cheap; drop/prod; state/teats, taste; wasp/paws, swap; priest/stripe; prides/spider; oils/soil

Test 4 (page 58)

Topic 19	**1.** world	**2.** worth	**3.** warder	**4.** warts
Topic 20	**5.** <u>The boy</u> (climbed) the tree.		**6.** <u>My cat</u> (likes) cream.	
	7. <u>Carpenters</u> (make) things from wood.		**8.** <u>Mr Douglas</u> (closed) the door.	
Topic 21	**9.** end	**10.** pie	**11.** eat/at	**12.** you
Topic 22	**13.** one	**14.** two	**15.** two	**16.** one
Topic 23	**17.** so	**18.** unless	**19.** until	**20.** before
Topic 24	**21–4.** deal/lead; warder/reward; slate/steal; blame/amble			